SURVIVE
and
THRIVE

Thrive!
Jamie

SURVIVE
and
THRIVE

How to
UNLOCK PROFITS
in a Startup with 1-10 Employees

LAURIE L. TAYLOR

Printed in the United States of America.

ISBN: 987-1503017245

This publication is designed to provide accurate and authoritative information in regard to the subject matter covered. It is sold with the understanding that the publisher is not engaged in rendering legal, accounting, or other professional services. If legal advice or other expert assistance is required, the services of a competent professional person should be sought.

TABLE OF CONTENTS

INTRODUCTION

The honeymoon is over. You have your startup capital, you've ramped up to four to six employees quickly and now the fun begins!

Getting out of the gate with a new company isn't easy, but it's a cakewalk compared to creating a consistently profitable business that you can run without it running you.

As companies grow, the complexity level of the organization increases. That complexity level doesn't increase because of revenues, profits or equity growth. Complexity increases because of the one factor in a company that is the hardest to control: people!

James Fischer, author of the 7 Stages of Growth and the book, *Navigating the Growth Curve*, discovered that as companies add more people to the equation, the dynamics change. Fischer developed the 7 Stages of Growth to address entrepreneurial companies struggling to manage growth, from 1 – 500 employees. I worked with him for five years as a managing partner at Origin Institute.

Through my current company, FlashPoint!, I have spoken to thousands of CEOs regarding the unique 7 Stages of Growth business model. The results are overwhelming. The information resonates with CEOs immediately.

> Complexity increases because of the one factor in a company that is the hardest to control: people!

At a recent presentation to over a hundred CEOs, a seasoned CEO, now running his twelfth company, said:

"After eighteen years of doing turnarounds and twelve years of investment banking, I finally found a system that prescribes the ideal management styles and focus for different sized companies. I am on the board of a private company and will be applying the Stages of Growth techniques when advising this company."

This reaction is typical from a CEO who has been around the block, who understands the challenges of growing a successful company and who understands that simply reading the next how-to, book of the month isn't a formula for building a successful company.

The 7 Stages of Growth gets CEO's attention because the concepts allow a business owner to do three things.

1. Predict how growth will impact them.
2. Get them focused on the right things at the right time.
3. Help leaders adapt to the necessary changes as the company grows.

This model allows you to look at the past, the present and the future in order to better understand what hidden agents are impacting your ability to grow. Once you identify those hidden agents, and put a name to the underlying issues, you can solve them and move on.

The 7 Stages of Growth provides every single employee the ability to understand the challenges a company faces as it grows. Each challenge can be talked about in terms everyone understands, thus taking the mystery out of running a company.

The impact of creating a "language of growth" starts with understanding that language doesn't *describe* a person's experience, it *defines* their experience. Change the language and you change the experience.

> *"As a successful but frustrated 15 year Stage 1 company we had tried many approaches to growth with limited success. It was clear we could survive but could we thrive? Laurie Taylor's extraordinary facilitation of the Growth Curve methodologies was excellent to help us understand what needed to be done. Having clarity is critical not only for a founder like myself but also the team that supports them and the business."*
>
> Jim Dryburg, CEO, The Balanced WorkLife Company

In talking with business owners every day, I know they struggle to keep their focus on the constant barrage of issues. A fast-growing enterprise can quickly grow beyond the owner's ability to manage everything.

This book is geared to address critical areas of focus for a Stage 1 company. You may not define growth by the addition of employees. You may think growth means creating a business that allows you to have a solid income for as long as you want it. Or, you may just be starting to consider the amazing possibilities your company has to offer and are looking for ways of managing it as you grow.

Because Fischer's model is built on the premise that says as you add people, you add complexity, a business owner has to make it a high priority to build the kind of environment that attracts, focuses and keeps talented employees. To that end, building a profitable company depends upon your ability to manage people.

The end result is yours to determine. You have taken the first step in developing a strong foundation by considering the research-proven concepts that support the 7 Stages of Growth enterprise development model. If your company continues to add employees, I hope you return to my websites often to learn more about the challenges of each of the 7 Stages of Growth.

I wish you success in growing your business!

Your success. My passion.

Laurie Taylor, President
FlashPoint! LLC
www.igniteyourbiz.com
www.destination-greatness.com
www.growthcurvespecialists.com

What a Stage 1 Company Looks Like

A Stage 1 company, or startup, has 1 – 10 employees. At this stage of growth, it's all about survival. A Stage 1 company is CEO-centric, meaning the CEO is the specialist who has created a product or service and is now getting his idea to take shape.

A Stage 1 company innovates quickly; it does not get locked into any one specific focus at the beginning. It should quickly discover, explore, experiment and find the right product or service that the company intends to bring out into the world.

As the CEO, 50% of your time should be spent as the technician or the specialist, while 10% of your time should be spent as a manager. The other 40% of your time should be spent creating and fine tuning the vision of the company. This percentage blend is also often referred to as the Three Faces of a Leader.

As a Stage 1 leader, don't worry about hitting the bulls-eye; just hit the target! You need to figure out how to generate income: cash flow is your number one challenge. At this stage of growth, trial and error is the name of the game. Your *risk* is *high* because there are still so many unknowns.

As a company navigates through Stage 1, its primary goal is to develop a business model that is profitable and sustainable. A CEO should evaluate how the company will grow and think about the following.

1. Value Proposition
2. Customers/Channel
3. Product/Service Features/Benefits
4. Revenue Model
5. Marketing and Sales Processes
6. Operations Process
7. Profitability
8. Cash Flow

In Stage 1, team selection is about how a staff member "fits" the culture and his ability to do whatever it takes to get the job done (specialized skills and experience are secondary).

The CEO's staff needs to help facilitate how work gets done and how quickly. The staff also needs to be flexible and willing to embrace change because there are so many unknowns and things can change quickly as the leader frequently makes adjustments to find what works best.

> **Cash flow is your number one challenge.**

REQUIRED LEADERSHIP SKILL BASE

- Identify one or more market opportunities.
- Construct a skeletal business plan.
- Raise sufficient capital.
- Provide a product or service.
- Determine what needs to be done and then do it.
- Serve in multiple roles at the same time.
- Have the ability to sell your product or service.
- Create a culture of accountability.

Creating and maintaining focus is very difficult in Stage 1. A high degree of uncertainty affects the CEO's ability to stay focused. Unless the business has outside funding, poor cash flow and limited capital can force leaders to prematurely stray from the original core business by chasing projects that might bring in money. A Stage 1 company needs to stay focused on its principal goals and objectives.

My promise to Stage 1 leaders, those of you running companies with 1 – 10 employees, or a fresh startup, is this:

If you embrace the 5 Challenges that I'm going to outline, take the time to study them and apply the knowledge I'll share with you, you will start to build a solid foundation for your company; whether you stay in Stage 1 or grow your business up to a Stage 7, with 161 – 500 employees.

> A Stage 1 company needs to stay focused on its principal goals and objectives.

How do I know? Because as the owner and partner of a multi-million dollar company that I helped grow from two to over one hundred employees, we struggled in Stage 1 for all of the reasons I'm going to cover with you here. And because we struggled, we lost critical traction and when you lose traction, you create even more chaos. We grew to over $12 million in sales. However, we would have grown to over $50 million in sales if I had known then what I know now.

HIDDEN AGENTS

WHAT IS A HIDDEN AGENT?

Hidden agents provide CEOs with a language to use to identify critical issues that may be creating obstacles to their growth. By understanding the hidden agents, a CEO can get to the root cause of a problem faster and engage their management team in helping identify the right issues.

In the 7 Stages of Growth series of books, I'll identify three critical hidden agents that a CEO must be aware of to improve performance, productivity and profitability and avoid losing traction.

HIDDEN AGENT #1: BUILDER/ PROTECTOR RATIO

More than likely, if you own a business, you understand a Builder mentality. You create new ideas, take on new initiatives and find ways to expand the revenue and profitability of your company. You choose to challenge and improve the way things are done, thrive on risk and are highly supportive of growth.

A Protector mindset is cautious and prefers to slow down the pace of change. They are risk averse and highly suspicious of growth. Protectors may not feel confident in the company's financial strength and are slow to embrace the optimism of the future.

Builder/Protector is a measurement within a company of confidence versus caution. This hidden agent measures the intensity and the balance between the state of confidence and the state of caution inherent in the psyche of an organization.

This measurement tool is critical for a CEO and their leadership team to be able to assess the company's ability to accept change and successfully navigate the change. React with confidence to that change and you help the company achieve its stated goals.

> There's a balance between Builders and Protectors that is critical to recognize.

A company's Builder/Protector Ratio will change based on its current stage of growth.

This hidden agent is expressed as a ratio such as 4 Builders to 1 Protector (4:1), which is the optimal Builder/Protector ratio during Stage 1. It simply means that based on your stage of growth, there's a balance between Builders and Protectors that is critical to recognize.

BUILDERS:

- Create new ideas.
- Take on new initiatives.
- Find ways to expand the revenue and profits.
- Challenge the way things are done.

- Are risk tolerant and highly supportive of growth.
- Are highly confident.
- Are always looking for new opportunities.
- Don't back down from everyday challenges.

PROTECTORS:

- Are cautious and slow paced.
- Are risk averse.
- May not feel confident in the company's financial strength.
- Tend to be suspicious of new markets.
- Prefer to apply the brakes (and should be encouraged to do so when appropriate).

Too much Protector, the company could stall. Too much Builder, the company could fail. Moving too slow or moving too fast will make management more difficult and the top executive will continually struggle to gain buy in.

The CEO must not only be a Builder, he must develop a team that, for the most part, is like-minded in order to persevere through the challenges of a startup. But, a bit of the Protector mindset is helpful to counter the Builders' tendency to be eternal optimists with tunnel vision.

> Too much Protector, the company could stall. Too much Builder, the company could fail.

WHAT IS TOO MUCH WHEN IT COMES TO THE BUILDER/PROTECTOR MINDSET?

While the results of a Builder mindset tend to manifest in ways that help a company grow (ability to drive sales, ability to look for new opportunities, strong financials), too much Builder mindset can create issues, just as a Protector mindset can restrict growth if applied too often or for prolonged periods of time.

SYMPTOMS OF TOO MUCH BUILDER:

1. Hockey stick sales projections.
2. Hiring in advance of need.
3. Taking on higher risk projects without proper reward.
4. Over-committing and under-delivering.
5. Lack of clarity in the direction of the company.

SYMPTOMS OF TOO MUCH PROTECTOR:

1. Unwilling to try new marketing and business development techniques.
2. Too much focus on expenses, not enough on revenue.
3. Sees hurdles instead of opportunities.
4. Insulated, not seeking divergent opinions.
5. Leaders seem fearful about the future and stop communicating.
6. The business is hesitant to embrace change.
7. Decisions take too long and opportunities are missed.

Understanding your company's Builder/Protector Ratio improves your insight into your company's mental health by:

1. Allowing you to measure the company's ability to meet and overcome challenges.
2. Communicating the company's willingness to perceive and take advantage of opportunities in its path.
3. Measuring the strength of the company's immune defense system, acting as a barrier against low morale and poor performance.
4. Assessing the company's willingness to advance itself through change.
5. Telegraphing the company's belief in its future.
6. Communicating the company's trust in its leaders.

WHEN THE BUILDER/PROTECTOR RATIO IS OUT OF ALIGNMENT

The Builder/Protector Ratio is a powerful concept and once a CEO and his team understands it, the dynamic in a management team, and ultimately a company, can change within weeks.

When the Builder/Protector Ratio is out of alignment, a CEO can send a signal to his team that he is not confident about the direction of the company, without even being aware of it. That lack of confidence will manifest in key employees or the management team, and ultimately ricochet throughout the entire company.

A Stage 1 company is CEO-centric, so if the CEO is overly cautious, he could unwittingly bring the company to a grinding halt. Confidence is critical in any stage of growth. In a startup however, if the Builder/Protector Ratio is less than 4:1, the company will not succeed. The Builder/Protector Ratio, often referred to as the Confidence/Caution Ratio, is one of the hidden agents uncovered in the 7 Stages of Growth research. As such, it should be a CEO's first consideration, especially if he sees his company pulling back instead of marching confidently forward.

HIDDEN AGENT #2: THREE FACES OF A LEADER

The 7 Stages of Growth research uncovered the Three Faces of a Leader. The length of time a leader spends wearing one of these faces depends upon their stage of growth. There is a model percentage blend for each stage.

For a Stage 1 company, the Three Faces blend looks like this:

VISIONARY: 40%

Visionary leaders ensure the company knows where it wants to go. They can take the most insignificant situation and turn it into an opportunity. It's important that leaders in Stage 1 are creating a vision that the employees can embrace. There is so much chaos and uncertainty with a Stage 1 company; a leader will provide confidence by making sure that vision is communicated to all employees, often.

> A leader will provide confidence by making sure that vision is communicated to all employees, often.

MANAGER: 10%

The manager face understands the importance of growing a company through the management of workflow and people. A manager creates order and focuses on pragmatic systems and procedures that make the company run well. He should strive to be emotionally intelligent and dedicated to helping people succeed. The manager face is low in Stage 1 because people are stepping up and getting things done. There isn't a need for too much structure or too many processes.

SPECIALIST: 50%

The specialist face immerses in the work the company produces. They understand the need to capture the necessary processes, to deliver the work and meet clients' needs. In most cases, the specialist is the person who came up with the idea to start the company; he is action oriented and detail focused.

All three faces are critical throughout the growing stages of a company.

WHEN THE THREE FACES OF A LEADER BLEND ARE OUT OF ALIGNMENT

A CEO of a growing company needs to bring all three faces (Visionary, Manager and Specialist) to the table every day. The three faces provide needed focus when a leader is working hard to transition his company from a CEO-centric mindset to an Enterprise-centric mindset. Essentially, the CEO needs to "let it go to let it grow."

In Stage 1, the leader is more than likely the Specialist, spending 50% of his time making sure the service or product the company is producing is functional and ready for prime time. Imagine if the

CEO spent too much time being Visionary and not enough time being the Specialist. Neglecting product or service development at this critical stage of growth could cause the company to lose steam, fade away or never make it out of Stage 1.

There is a fine line between the amounts of time the CEO should spend being a Specialist and a Visionary (50% vs 40%), but that 10% difference will show up on the company's bottom line as it moves into Stage 2. Take the time to focus on the processes that make the company's product or service a winner. Understanding and balancing the three faces of a leader helps a CEO in Stage 1 succeed.

HIDDEN AGENT #3: LEADERSHIP STYLE

Leaders create resonance in an organization by ensuring that the entire fabric of a company is laced with emotional intelligence. Developing a new leadership style means changing how one operates with other people.

To succeed, leadership development must be the strategic priority of the enterprise. There are six defined leadership styles utilized in the 7 Stages of Growth. Those styles are explained in Daniel Goleman's book, *Primal Leadership*. The six styles are: Visionary, Coaching, Affiliative, Democratic, Commanding and Pacesetting.

Understanding the six leadership styles and how they impact each stage of growth is a powerful tool for any CEO. In the 7 Stages of Growth enterprise development model, there are three critical leadership styles for each stage of growth and they are stacked in order of importance. The Primary Style is the most effective and should be used the most, followed by the Secondary Style and then the Auxiliary Style. All three bring different dynamics to a CEO's management world and the more a CEO understands when to apply each style the more effective he will be.

> When people understand how their job fits into the bigger picture, they have clarity.

For a Stage 1 leader, the top leadership style is Visionary, followed by Coaching, followed by Commanding. A successful leader of a Stage 1 company must be able to bring all three leadership styles into play but the Visionary style is the most effective.

When you are utilizing a Visionary style, you are strongly driving the emotional climate upwards and transforming the spirit of the organization. This is accomplished by articulating where the company is going, not how it will get there. You allow people the opportunity to innovate, think and apply their knowledge. When people understand how their job fits into the bigger picture, they have clarity. You are able to create shared goals, which builds team commitment.

Visionary leaders retain talented people, offer them a unique brand and help them understand the "why." The ability to be transparent is critical and visionary leaders understand that distributing knowledge is the secret to success.

Coaching, the Secondary Style for Stage 1, is the most effective of all the leadership styles and the least used. The Coaching style helps people identify their unique strengths and weaknesses, and ties them to their personal and career goals. Coaches are good at delegating, a critical skill that will define how quickly the company grows beyond the leader's influence. A Coaching style works best with employees who show initiative. A group of self-motivated people is the best defense against the chaos that is so prevalent in Stage 1.

Of the six leadership styles, four of them are resonant, meaning they boost performance, while two are dissonant, meaning they should be applied with caution. The Commanding style is considered one of the dissonant styles and despite its negative inclination, the command-and-control style can be effective when used sparingly. A CEO may need to engage this style if the company experiences a crisis that requires someone to step up and quickly direct activities to avoid disaster. When swift change is necessary to forestall a financial downturn, the leader has to act forcefully to turn the ship around.

WHEN LEADERSHIP STYLE IS OUT OF ALIGNMENT

The ability to effectively utilize all six leadership styles is what distinguishes an emotionally aware leader from a leader who elects to focus more on tasks than people. Stage 1 leaders tend to gravitate toward the Commanding or Pacesetting leadership styles. Business owners feel a tremendous sense of urgency when launching a new product or service. That urgency forces the leader to be more direct and there can be a tendency to micro-manage in this early stage. A Commanding or Pacesetting style may work in the short term but not in the long term.

However, because a CEO in Stage 1 is hiring for "fit" and bringing in people who believe in what he is doing, the Visionary style is very important. By leading with vision and helping each new hire buy into how the product or service will impact the clients, that leader is laying a critical foundation for the company's future.

By understanding all six of the leadership styles and adjusting their leadership style to each stage of growth, a CEO will be better prepared for the changes that come as the company adds employees.

PREDICTING GROWTH

When I present the 7 Stages of Growth to CEOs around the country, I know two things.

1. If you are starting a company or running a company you are smart, energetic, capable, able to think outside the box, willing to put in long hours, have a strong vision, believe 150% in your product or service and feel overwhelmed most of the time.

2. You'd like a structure that you can utilize to help you figure out what is coming, how to manage the hundreds of issues that you deal with every day and how to make sure you survive to the next stage of your business's growth cycle.

I can't change who you are, but I can, I guarantee, give you a structure that will help you accomplish three things.

1. Figure out why you are struggling to stay focused.
2. Show you that you can predict how growth will impact you.
3. Help you understand what you need to do to adapt to the changes your company is going through.

This book is designed to help a Stage 1 CEO understand where to focus his energies in order to get the most traction as he starts to build a successful company.

A CEO's ability to get clear about the right things at the right time is what separates high performing companies from mediocre companies. The small percentage of companies that succeed are the ones that tend to stay ahead of their growth curve.

When James Fischer interviewed growth-smart companies in his 7 Stages of Growth research study, he was able to identify 27 specific challenges that business owners experienced as they grew their companies. Business owners find value in these 27 challenges because they finally have a starting point to talk about what's going on in their businesses.

It's hard for business owners, bombarded by issues every day, to articulate what is going on for them. They know something is creating a problem, but they can't identify what it is. The 27 Challenges help put a name to what business owners are experiencing. That's a big step when you are trying to engage a team of people to help you fix something.

> A CEO's ability to get clear about the right things at the right time is what separates high performing companies from mediocre companies.

Digging deeper, I'm going to identify the Top 5 Challenges for your current stage of growth. I'll provide insight into how to use that knowledge and apply it to your business, so you can stay ahead of your own growth curve.

THE 27 CHALLENGES

1. Profits are inadequate to grow the company
2. Need for an improved profit design
3. Customers are migrating away from products/ services
4. Continual cash flow challenges
5. Limited capital available to grow
6. Employee turnover
7. Hiring quality staff
8. Staff morale and voltage challenges
9. Need for a flexible planning model
10. Need to have better staff buy-in
11. Project management and resource coordination challenges
12. Leadership/staff communication gap
13. New staff orientation
14. Staff training
15. Unclear values throughout the organization
16. Dealing with the cost of lost expertise or knowledge when employees leave
17. Chaotic periods destabilize company
18. Organization needs to understand how the company will grow in the future, not just the leadership
19. Organization needs to better understand the impact that staff satisfaction has on the company's profitability
20. Company culture is generally resistant to change

21. The marketplace and your customers change too quickly
22. Difficulty forecasting problem areas before they surface
23. Difficulty diagnosing the real problems or obstacles to growth
24. Too slow getting new products/services to market
25. Not able to quickly get systems and procedures in place as the company is growing
26. Weak product/service development and differentiation in market
27. Expanding sales

THE TOP 5 CHALLENGES OF A STAGE 1 COMPANY

Throughout the stages of growth model, we guide CEOs on how to prioritize time, energy and dollars. Focusing on the right things at the right time will accelerate growth.

THE TOP 5 CHALLENGES FOR A STAGE 1 COMPANY, IN THIS ORDER, ARE:

1. Cash flow
2. Chaotic periods destabilize the company
3. Too slow getting new products/services to market
4. Limited capital to grow
5. Expanding sales

Challenge #1:
Cash Flow

Knowing that cash flow issues will be a challenge is a big part of your job as the CEO of a Stage 1 company. Having a plan to address this critical challenge will keep you ahead of your growth curve.

Cash is cash and revenue is revenue. They are not the same thing. More than one company has closed its doors drowning in revenue, unable to pay the bills. Managing cash flow means understanding how much money a company has every day or every week to pay the bills, which is paramount to keeping the company afloat.

A company never has too little cash to track. Business leaders who believe they'll start tracking cash when they have some don't understand the reality of cash flow management.

There is nothing more important than understanding how fast the cash is coming in (or not) and how fast cash is leaving the business. In fact, understanding cash flow can help leaders make better decisions up to six months in advance.

By paying close attention to how cash is flowing in and out of the business, a CEO can leverage even a small amount of cash, and sometimes, in the early stages of any business, that's all there is!

I'm going to address two approaches that I promise will stem your cash flow issues. All you have to do is implement them!

EXERCISE #1:

CREATING YOUR PROFIT PLAN

A profit plan is simply a budget. People react negatively to the concept of budgeting, so I prefer this more proactive term. After all, that's what running a business is all about! So why not *plan* to be *profitable*?

The art of projecting how much income you will generate each month, how much it will cost you to produce your product or service each month and how much it will take to run your business each month is my definition of a profit plan.

> What you
> don't know
> **will** hurt you.

Start right away and create your own. If you are new to this concept, start with your overhead expenses. Project your monthly expenses on an excel spreadsheet for twelve months. Credit card payments go here. Loan payments go here. Rent or mortgage payments go here.

Add it up. If you just want to break even in your business, the number you come up with for your expenses is the amount of income you have to generate every month. If you want to make money, you have to bring in more money than you spend.

What you don't know *will* hurt you. In this case, the more you know about what it takes to run your business, the more successful you will be. A profit plan is simply a way to help you make better decisions and to keep you focused on what it will take to make money.

Profit Planning Work Sheet

To learn more about your profit plan and to download your own spreadsheet, go to http://bit.ly/bizchallenges

The key to my definition is the word *monthly*. This is about projecting by the month, how much income you are going to bring into your business and how much you are going to spend to keep the business going.

While all business owners need to understand their Profit & Loss statement, remember, your P&L comes out at the end of each month. While it is good to know what happened in a previous month, it's too late to make any changes. A profit plan is a dynamic planning tool. It allows you to proactively make changes half way through the month if things aren't going the way you expected or are going better than you expected.

THE VALUE OF A PROFIT PLAN

Every business, no matter how small, should track their income and expenses monthly. If you don't, you are simply winging it. You have no idea where you made money and no idea where you spent money.

If you spend 70% of your time focused on driving top line revenue and 30% on the expense side of your business, you will start to see an impact on your bottom line profitability.

All too often, business owners get caught up in managing the costs of their business. It's easy to refrain from certain activities when money is tight, especially when it comes to large ticket items such as building a website, marketing materials and staff training. Remember, if an activity is going to generate money, make it a priority.

If you invest the time and expend the energy to know what it takes to land the next client, make the next sale, send out that new proposal; you will constantly keep yourself focused on driving top line revenue.

Cash Flow For (account): _FlashPoint!_
Week of: Monday _Aug. 18_ **to Friday** _Aug. 22_

Balance in bank as of _Aug.18_ $ _15,000_
Date   Cash in Bank

Add in Receivables:

Date	Customer/Source	Amount	Transfer/Deposit Date
Aug 19	Deposit for Training	$ 1500.00	Aug. 20
Aug 19	Deposit for Speaking	$ 2500.00	Aug. 20
Aug 21	Monthly coaching	$ 500.00	Aug. 21
Aug 22	Monthly coaching	$ 500.00	Aug. 21
		$	
		$	
		$	
		$	
		$	
Total Receivables		$ 5,000.00	

$ _20,000.00_
Total Cash In Bank

Deduct Payables:

Date	Vendor/Bill	Amount	Date Paid
Aug.18	Amer.Express credit card	$ 1,000.00	
Aug.20	Website upgrade	$ 500.00	
Aug.22	Loan payment	$ 350.00	
		$	
		$	
		$	
		$	
		$	
		$	
Total Payables		$ 1,850.00	

Balance in Bank by _Aug.22_ : $ _18,150.00_
Date   Total Cash

Outline the specific activities that will keep you focused on driving revenue every day and then devote at least 70% of each day to bringing money in the door. Creating and managing your own profit plan allows you to proactively stay ahead of downturns in your business. If you start to see revenues slow down in June, you can adjust by slowing down expenditures and beefing up your sales.

If you aren't tracking your revenues and expenses by the month, you are keeping all the numbers in your head and running on gut instinct. While this might work when times are good (although I don't advocate it), it is a disaster waiting to happen when facing a tough economy or a downturn in business.

> Stop wishing for profits and start planning for profits!

EXERCISE #2:

MONITORING AND MANAGING CASH

Here's an exercise you should practice to generate income and protect your cash.

Use the following formula:

1. Select the period of time you want to track your cash.
2. Take the amount of cash you have in the bank.
3. Subtract any payables for that period of time.
4. Add in any receivables for that same period of time.
5. What you have left is your cash on hand.

Cash Flow For (account): _____
Week of: Monday _____ **to Friday** _____

Balance in bank as of _____ $ _____
Date   Cash in Bank

Add in Receivables:

Date	Customer/Source	Amount	Transfer/Deposit Date
		$	
		$	
		$	
		$	
		$	
		$	
		$	
		$	
		$	
		$	
Total Receivables		$	

$ _____
Total Cash In Bank

Deduct Payables:

Date	Vendor/Bill	Amount	Date Paid
		$	
		$	
		$	
		$	
		$	
		$	
		$	
		$	
		$	
		$	
Total Payables		$	

Balance in Bank by _____ : $ _____
Date   Total Cash

You only count money that you know is coming in during that period and you only track money that is going out during that period. If you *think* it's coming in, don't count it.

Also, don't assume you are out of the woods when your business starts to generate income. As the owner, cash flow management will always be a part of your job and you should always know where you stand.

As the CEO, you *have* to understand the financials. You can't give that responsibility away to anyone, especially in a Stage 1 company. Yes, you can hire a book-keeper to set up your books, pay people, send out invoices and collect receivables. No, you don't have to do *every-thing* when managing your financials.

> As the owner, cash flow management will always be a part of your job.

However, *you do have to know everything* about the financial health of your company. CEOs who abdicate this responsibility usually don't get the traction they need. I know CEOs who decided they didn't want anything to do with the bookkeeping side of their business and ended up in debt because payroll taxes were never paid or taxes were never filed.

A CEO who doesn't take a strong and serious interest in the book-keeping side of his business is asking for trouble. Know where your money is going. Know who is paying and who isn't. Know how much money is in the bank. Know how much you need to bring in to make a profit. Know what your profit goals are.

Practice cash flow planning. Tracking it weekly will help you understand the ups and downs of your business and be focused on the movement of cash in your business.

THE VALUE OF MANAGING CASH

The real value in managing cash flow is that it provides a realistic picture. You can't *wish* money in the door. You may have to push out some payables if your receivables are weak for that period of time.

By managing your cash flow, you eliminate surprises. Cash flow projection allows you to stay focused on the one activity you should prioritize: following the money!

A business owner who is passionate about the financial aspects of his company will always have a company to be passionate about.

For help in creating a profit plan, managing cash flow and selecting key indicators, take a look at my online program, *Destination, Greatness: Your Financial Success System*, which will provide all the tools and information you need to be a financially aware leader. You can read more about it at www.destination-greatness.com.

RESOLVING THE CHALLENGE OF CASH FLOW

Cash is the lifeblood of every business, no matter how big or how small. Having money is not a guarantee that you will be able to keep money.

A planned approach to generate, protect and save cash for the business should be a CEO's top priority.

At some point in your company's first stage of growth, you will need more cash. You've heard the statement, "Get your money from the bank when you *don't* need it." If you know you are going to have need of large sums of cash to buy equipment or expand to another location, or if you work with larger businesses that pay slowly, you want to create a relationship with your banker to set up a credit line *before* you need the money. Having a credit line is a sign of a smart business owner. As long as you are diligent in keeping the credit line under control, it can be a huge asset when growth opportunities appear.

One pitfall in managing cash is clients who pay late or who don't pay at all. Make sure you have a handle on receivables and if a client is slow in paying you, evaluate your relationship and keep a good handle on how much work you are doing for him. You may need to stop work until he catches up or hold products until he's paid the account in full.

> Set up a credit line **before** you need the money.

Cash flow is an indicator of a business's health and success. When you have a handle on your cash flow, you make better decisions. And making good decisions is just better for your business.

Challenge #2: Chaotic Periods Destabilize Your Company

A CEO must:

- Love chaos.
- Be a good learner.
- Be able to put his or her ego aside.
- Be ready to learn from mistakes.
- Understand that the same mistake may be made more than once.

If you can't embrace these concepts, you may be better off working for someone else. Ouch. I'm sorry if that isn't what you want to hear but the reality of running a business is *you*, the business owner, *have to embrace chaos,* especially in the early years. If you try and control the chaos, you will be miserable and you will make everyone that works for you miserable also.

A Stage 1 company is still figuring itself out. Chances are you started your company because you were very good at *something*. You felt you could do something better than others, you were extremely good at something and you wanted to help others. Or you knew there was a need in the market and you set out to address it. There are as many reasons people start businesses, as there are businesses in this world.

To embrace chaos as a Stage 1 owner, you must recognize that you need proof of concept. You need to test your product or service. You need to build rapport with potential clients so they will buy you and what you're offering. To do that, you need to become very good at understanding problems and you need to understand how what you offer solves those problems.

If you get stuck too early on a certain way of doing business, or you think there is only one way to set up your product or service, or you assume that you know what your prospects want, you will lose traction, waste a lot of money, time and energy and eventually burn out.

> You must recognize that you need proof of concept.

EXERCISE #1:

COMMUNICATE CRITICAL INFORMATION – OFTEN

Effective and intentional communication will be your best friend as you navigate your way through chaotic periods of destabilization.

Here are 10 questions that will reduce chaos and engage your employees.

1. What does the organization want to become in the future?

Take the time to explore this with your team. Find out how they think about growth and the potential they see for your company. This may evolve as you move from one stage of growth to another. That's good! A company is a dynamic, living breathing entity.

2. In what area does the company really excel?

Your greatest asset when answering this question lies with your customers. Find opportunities to engage them in conversation about how they view your value. Ask them what makes you unique. Why do they like working with you? You may think it's because of your product or service, but you many find they like your ability to think ahead of their needs and appreciate that you are always looking out for them.

3. What does the company offer that the market wants or needs?

Remember, we are talking about engaging your employees in conversations that give them a sense of control over different aspects of the company. Having them better understand why you are unique and why your customers love your products or services builds pride in your employees. When they believe what they do has an impact on others, they will become more engaged in making sure they stay ahead of those market needs.

4. **Why do people want to work for the company?**

   "We pay better than our competitors" is a shortsighted answer to a much more complicated question. Making a good living is important for any employee. However, there has to be something more than just getting a paycheck for your employees to be engaged and to be excited to come to work every day. The answer lies in how you view them. Do you value them as individuals or are they simply cogs in a wheel? (This one you can't fake.) When people feel valued, their attitude shifts and they become the kind of employee you love to have around. Make sure you know the answer to this question and make sure everyone else in the company knows it as well.

5. **What are the company's values?**

   Undefined values that are not written down are simply ideas about how people should act. That leads to expectations that are never met, frustration on the part of managers and burn out on the part of employees. Your values are critical to your business. Define them. Make them easy to remember. Talk about them. Reward people when you see them practicing those values with co-workers or customers. Values tell your employees what behaviors you encourage and what behaviors you won't tolerate. Don't leave this up to your employees to figure out as they go. They will get discouraged early on and the good ones will leave.

6. What types of behaviors are encouraged?

Be specific! Going the extra mile for a customer. Helping a new employee feel welcome. Improving leadership skills. Dealing with conflict in an upfront manner without letting anger create bigger issues. Being accountable. Owning up to mistakes. Identifying areas where the company can improve a process.

7. What kind of behaviors are discouraged?

Again, be specific. Sending angry text or email messages back and forth. Glossing over a customer's concern for any reason. Lack of follow through. Allowing cliques to form that cause other employees to feel uneasy. Is gossip allowed to flourish? Is it okay for employees to show up late for meetings?

8. Why is the company experiencing chaos today?

When chaos is felt in an organization, it's felt first at the front line; whatever that looks like for your company. Chaos in the grocery store at the checkout stand can be the result of not enough checkout lines available for the number of shoppers and no one to bag groceries. The checkout people will feel the chaos long before the manager, who's in his office in the back. Where does your company feel chaos first? How have you prepared your employees to identify that chaos? What does it feel like? How is it addressed? Talking about chaos is the first line of defense. Don't ignore the conversation. Find out how chaos looks in your company and take steps to manage it proactively.

9. Why is it a good thing to have chaos?

A little bit of chaos can keep a company focused. As in nature, chaos is critical for growth. The caterpillar goes through a difficult transition to become a butterfly. In the chrysalis stage, the caterpillar starts to change and change quickly. If anything interrupts this stage of transition the butterfly will never develop. It will die. Chaos is needed in nature and in organizations to keep us growing and developing. A leader's main job is to help his organization walk the line between equilibrium and chaos every day. Too much equilibrium and the company will slow to a stop. Too much chaos and it can spin out of control. The best approach to chaos is to talk about it. Let people vent their frustrations when things seem too hectic. Allow chaos to exist with an understanding of what it is and how it can be controlled.

10. What can we do to minimize the impact that chaos has on us?

Talk about it! Share what's going on in the organization that appears on the surface as chaotic. Then, drill down to solutions that keep people from feeling uncomfortable or nervous. Allow them to think proactively of ways to address the chaos. In the early stages of growth, you have to embrace chaos because of the uncertainty going on around you. In later stages of growth, you have to look at the cause of the chaos, which could be from a lack of processes. Engage employees to be detectives, find out what the problems are and encourage them to find solutions and share them with the company. Chaos is difficult to deal with when it's ignored. The best defense against chaos is a solid offense.

Address these questions early on in Stage 1 of your business and your life will be much easier as you grow.

THE VALUE OF COMMUNICATION

Don't allow chaos to destabilize your company. Chaotic times will always exist; it's how you cope with them that will allow you to grow and move forward. All of the challenges in Stage 1 need to be dealt with or else they will follow the CEO into the next stage of growth.

Four rules govern the 7 Stages of Growth:

Rule 1: The movement from one stage of growth to another begins as soon as you land in any stage of growth.

Rule 2. What you don't get done in a specific stage of growth does not go away.

Rule 3. Time will make a difference.

Rule 4. If you aren't growing, you're dying.

This challenge is related to how a business leader thinks about the company. With fewer than eleven employees, the company is still CEO-centric. As the CEO brings people on board and the company starts to grow, he will need to help the staff understand the realities of running a business.

Many times, employees who have worked for larger organizations join the company. They come from a well-defined culture with well-defined processes, roles and responsibilities. Employees joining a company that is in the early stages of growth need to be educated on the realities of working for a Stage 1 company.

Engaging your employees in identifying and defining your company's own processes, roles and responsibilities allows them to be truly invested. They have directly contributed to the company culture, and will feel valued as a result.

EXERCISE #2:

TALK ABOUT SUCCESSES AND FAILURES

Don't be afraid to talk about successes and failures with your small and loyal team. People who join a company early on in its lifecycle do so because of one factor: *you*, the business owner.

They get caught up in your *vision*, your *passion* and your *energy* and they want to be a part of that. Address the following questions often.

1. What is the company's vision today?

Find opportunities to talk about how you are fulfilling on your vision with specific examples. People love stories! Find examples that include a recent exchange with a prospect, how they became a client and how landing that contract helped move your company toward your vision.

> **Your staff doesn't expect you to be right all the time.**

Remind people where the company was a year or two years ago. After struggling to identify a vision, you finally did, and that's what helped the company focus on the products or services it's offering today.

Remember, your staff doesn't expect you to be right all the time. They do expect, however, that you will be transparent and authentic and above all, human. Don't disappoint. Share the good stories and the not so good stories and help everyone understand what it takes to be successful.

2. How well do people understand how their job fits into the overall vision?

Even in an early stage company, when people are pitching in to help with a myriad of activities, it's important that people understand how **what** they do fits into **why** they are doing it.

Help each person see the value. Later on, when roles and responsibilities are more defined, you will be ahead of the game. You will have spent time identifying activities, putting a value to them and helping people understand how that activity either a.) reduced chaos, b.) added to the bottom line, c.) identified a problem or d.) produced a critical process.

This one practice will pay you back in spades as your company grows.

3. How is information communicated throughout the organization?

With 1 – 10 employees, sharing critical information is not that hard. Usually meetings are effective and focused and people are engaged. However, creating a structure for meetings allows people to learn good habits. Having an agenda, asking people to show up on time, capturing critical points made, asking people to be accountable and reporting back on what they agreed to do and making sure everyone is heard are all good practices to ensure solid communication. Other effective communication strategies include establishing email protocol (let people know they should never have a negative conversation via email), showing people how to embrace conflict and proactively handle touchy issues.

4. What is the process to create the annual profit plan (budget)?

There is no better time to instigate open book management than in Stage 1. If you want to learn more about this powerful program, pick up Jack Stack's book, *The Great Game of Business*. If you are not inclined to fully embrace this approach, start small. Invite input from employees on cost-saving ideas; things they can impact such as reducing waste, energy-saving steps, being mindful of tools, equipment and supplies. Help them understand what it costs to run your business every month and the difference between revenue (sales coming in) and cash (money available to use).

Making a profit in a business doesn't require magic, but employees often wonder why they are told they can't do something because "it costs too much," when they know the company just landed a hundred thousand dollar contract. Help them to connect the dots.

5. What is the company's value proposition today?

A critical aspect of helping your employees understand what your company stands for is to show them how your value proposition helps differentiate you from your competitors. In many situations, employees aren't aware of the company's value proposition.

What is yours? Can you articulate it? Do you use your value proposition to help explain to employees why you are better/different than your competitors? Do you talk to your customers to find out what they say about your products or services? Are you effective at talking about the benefits of your offerings?

In this global economy it's important that you find ways to help your employees and your customers know the value your company brings to the table.

Value proposition tips from entrepreneur and conversion optimization expert, Peep Laia:

- Give your offering relevancy to customers by saying (outright) what problem it solves, or how it will improve their current situation.
- Quantify the value for your customers by listing specific benefits (steer clear of "It'll save you money," and opt instead for "You'll save $30/ month on your phone bill.")
- Place priority on your point of difference, which is the reason why your solution is better than the competition's in some notable way.

In Stage 1, it's possible you are still figuring this out. Great! Talk about it. Start this conversation with your employees. Don't assume people know the answers!

THE VALUE IN MANAGING CHAOS

Explaining to employees that open communication about what is and isn't effective is critical. In doing so, the leader will lessen the feelings that chaos brings. Chaos is unavoidable, but its impact can be minimized.

In many situations, uncontrolled chaos creates fear, uncertainty, second-guessing and a loss of confidence. The value in working to keep chaos somewhat controlled is in benefits such as improved performance and engaged employees.

In organizational behavioral studies, it has been shown that when new ways of doing things are introduced, it's hard for people to act in new ways just because they are told to do so. It's easy for people to revert back to the old ways of doing things, especially when they feel tense or confused.

> Empower employees to embrace chaos instead of allowing it to take over.

Because a Stage 1 company is constantly looking for new ways of doing things and discovering what works and what doesn't, it's easy for confusion to exist. The leader's ability to help employees stay alert to that tension can decrease the impact of chaos. Empower employees to embrace chaos instead of allowing it to take over and overwhelm them.

The chaos that is such a defining aspect of your company's foundation building in Stage 1 will provide you clarity as you grow.

RESOLVING THE CHALLENGE OF CHAOS

Chaos can help people gain new insights and force them to rethink how things work or don't work. As a Stage 1 leader, you want to allow yourself and your employees to "figure it out as you go," at least for a period of time, as you gain confidence in what you sell.

In Margaret Wheatley's book, *Finding Our Way: Leadership for an Uncertain Time*, she asks leaders to allow for open conversations and suggests these key questions when managing in chaotic times.

- Who's missing?
- Who else needs to do this work?
- Is the meaning of the work still clear?
- Is it changing?
- Are we becoming more truthful with each other?
- Is information becoming more open and easier to access?
- What are we learning about partnering with confusion and chaos?

Let your employees know you don't have all the answers and let

> Communicate often. Communicate consistently. Communicate honestly.

them help you find those answers. Communicate often. Communicate consistently. Communicate honestly. By talking about chaos, it will become a friend instead of an obstacle, and it will help you navigate to the next stage of growth.

Challenge #3: Too Slow Getting Your Products or Services to Market

There is a rhythm to running a business. The better you are at managing cash flow and chaos, the better you will be at getting your products or services to market. This particular challenge is a survival issue for a Stage 1 company, and a profitability issue for companies in the later stages of growth.

Regardless of the size of company, this challenge relates to three important issues.

1. Your employees don't understand the urgency of getting products or services to market.
2. There are broken processes or the processes are not being followed correctly.

3. There is a lack of training on the processes.

You might say the company needs to move faster to get its products or services to market. However, speed isn't always better.

When employees buy into the company's performance standards and understand the financial and customer satisfaction goals behind the delivery of that product or service, it's easier to stay on top of this challenge.

EXERCISE #1:

Ask yourself:

- Are assumptions being made about work processes?
- Do managers encourage employees to look for areas of improvement?
- Do all employees understand the bigger picture as to delivering on time?
- How do you share successes?
- Is there a reward mechanism in place to encourage systems improvements?

Taking a page from Jack Welch's book, *Jack: Straight from the Gut*, questions not only need to be asked, questions need to influence change. The issues that arise from those questions need to be turned into usable ideas, which is not an easy bridge to make. Ideas are a dime a dozen. It's the implementation of ideas that creates traction, improves morale and increases the bottom line.

To identify issues, you have to create a culture in which fear doesn't exist. CEOs and managers often ask, "Why don't they just tell me what's wrong? I never knew they were struggling with that process!" People won't tell you what's wrong if your reaction is to sigh, roll your eyes, cross your arms, release a long breath through clenched teeth, seem agitated and ask, "Why didn't you just fix it?" You know exactly what I'm talking about!

> Questions not only need to be asked, questions need to influence change.

Be approachable and open. Your body language telegraphs more feelings than words. When employees see negative body language, they shut down. It's your job to encourage employees to look under the surface of issues to identify what the real problems are. Encourage them to talk to others about what they see, gather input, challenge the status quo and then collaborate to come up with solutions.

Most businesses run on an impatient time clock. Remember the old adage, "If you had time to do it over again, you had time to do it right the first time." In the chaos of getting that project done on time, solving the customer's problem, revamping a process, training a new employee, hiring the right employee; we overlook the immediate slowdowns in favor of chaos and we tell ourselves we'll fix it or do it later.

Here are a few questions to ask in order to help employees understand that you want their input, you value it, and without their input, things won't change and chaos will rule.

- What are the major frustrations you deal with on a daily basis that you or your immediate manager can confront?
- What are the three best things about the company?
- What don't you like about how things are running?
- What changes would you like to see?

By creating a culture that encourages sound thinking, that takes those good ideas and uses the creative energy of each employee to see those ideas implemented, you'll create an environment that embraces change. Reward employees for innovative thinking and collaborative meetings where issues are discussed and solutions uncovered. Create an easy to use online reporting system that employees can use to identify problems with processes or call attention to where duplication of effort exists.

THE VALUE OF DEFINED WORK PROCESSES

The challenge of being too slow getting your products or services to market has many fingers. If a business owner takes time in the early stage of his company's development to focus on critical processes, the foundation is in place to ramp up quicker. The reality is those processes will and should change as you grow.

Create the mindset in your company that it's every single person's responsibility to hone in on, report on and help solve process issues

> Uncovering problems should be everyone's concern.

from the beginning. You will separate the wheat from the chaff; meaning you will edge out competitors and impact your bottom line faster.

Getting product out the door or making sure services are delivered has to be every employee's responsibility. This only happens if the CEO sends a clear and consistent message that process improvements are a part of the culture; uncovering problems should be everyone's concern.

EXERCISE #2:

GET CREATIVE ABOUT TRAINING OPPORTUNITIES

It's not easy to find or make time to train employees, especially while dealing with daily chaos. However, insufficient training can kill a company before it even gets a chance to get off the ground.

Early stage companies tend to lean toward philosophies such as "learn as you go," "trial by fire" or "get it or get out." Creating a culture that trains employees to think about ways to learn and shows them the value in teaching others will pay off every time. It doesn't require a huge investment in outside training programs. Tap into the intelligence of your people and challenge them to create lunch and learns, afternoon collaboration sessions or to share their ideas in an online forum.

Bring training conversations into every interaction and encourage your employees to do the same.

What did we learn last week?

How did that change impact our quality?

Where do we continue to see problems?

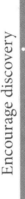

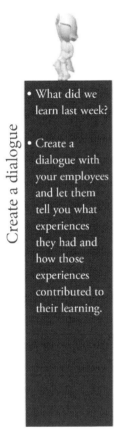

Create a dialogue

- What did we learn last week?

- Create a dialogue with your employees and let them tell you what experiences they had and how those experiences contributed to their learning.

Encourage discovery

- How did that change impact our quality?

- Sometimes the improvements are not evident when processes or people change. Encourage your employees to dig deeper than a surface review of how something impacted the quality of your product or service.

Ongoing communication

- Where do we continue to see problems?

- When you create a culture of communication, problems get identified sooner, get solved quicker and people feel good about seeing their improvements make a difference.

THE VALUE OF TRAINING

Training isn't a short-term project; it's about creating systems that people can use to be successful time and time again. Achieving excellence isn't nearly as impactful as *sustaining* excellence over time. Training literally means: *to direct the growth of,* (and even more important) *to teach so as to make fit, qualified or proficient.* Many businesses fail to look at the goal of training as a strategic differentiator. They just can't find the time to train people but somehow they can find the time to redo work, lose money, upset customers and lose great employees.

When you fail to train your people, your competitors win every time. Well-trained employees feel good about themselves because they know what's expected of them and they have the tools and the resources they need to do a great job. When your employees feel good about themselves, your customers feel their confidence.

> When you fail to train your people, your competitors win every time.

A Stage 1 company that makes staff training a priority will gain an advantage in the marketplace. Is there a good reason to ignore this critical aspect of growing your business?

RESOLVING THE CHALLENGE OF BEING TOO SLOW GETTING PRODUCTS OR SERVICES TO MARKET

Coming up with an idea and turning that idea into a business is hard work. It's at the core of why so many businesses fail in the first five years. Addressing the issues behind why your company is struggling with this challenge should be a high priority.

Make sure you are visible. People want to see and interact with the CEO. They want to hear from you. They love having the chance to talk with you. Walk around. Talk with people. Find out what's on their minds.

Take the time to make sure each person in your company understands how your company makes and keeps money. Help employees see how what they do every day impacts the business's ability to be successful.

There is no better time than Stage 1 to create training programs that every employee has a hand in developing. You will never be this close to your employees and customers again. This is the time to put procedures in place that help uncover problems in how products or services get delivered. Use this critical stage of growth to solidify an environment of learning, discovery and communication. A culture of commitment and engagement around solving problems should be fostered early in an organization.

Challenge #4: Limited Capital to Grow

The need to have enough operating capital, as well as investment capital, changes based on what stage of growth a company is in and what the long-term vision is for growth. Limited capital to grow is an issue whether the company delivers a product or a service. It is vital, in the early stages of a business, to take the time to get a handle on what resources are needed to grow.

Too often, CEOs are of the mindset, "If I just work hard, I'll succeed." There is a tendency for leaders to be short sighted when it comes to evaluating the amount of money the company will need to get off to a solid start and remain viable as growth occurs.

EXERCISE #1:

IDENTIFY YOUR CAPITAL NEEDS

Have you identified your capital needs? Have you created a profit plan?

Map out how you see your company growing. Do the brainwork that forces you to evaluate whether or not you can make the business successful.

Put your ideas down on paper. Think short and long term. If this turns into a business plan, great! Then, track your success every month. Check your assumptions before you spend money. Ask yourself if the outgo of money will produce an income of money. Of course there are things you will need to buy that don't give you an immediate return on your investment. I still maintain that you need to be able to justify those things and then show the return in order to stay ahead of problems.

THE VALUE OF IDENTIFYING YOUR CAPITAL NEEDS

Regardless of how you get your startup money, it's important for profitability to know in advance how that money will be spent.

Put together a solid profit plan and use this exercise to hold your feet to the fire in terms of seeing a return on that investment every month. If you run headlong into a business without a plan of how you are going to spend your money, you will run out before you see results.

EXERCISE #2:

IDENTIFY YOUR STARTUP FUNDING OUTLETS

Capital availability to a Stage 1 company often determines success or failure. The SBA, the Kauffman Foundation and your local banker will attest that the number one reason new business fail is because they lack capital.

So, you're a Stage 1 company and you don't have a rich relative or partner to stake your near-term capital needs. What are your best pathways to securing the appropriate startup seed funds necessary?

> The number one reason new businesses fail is because they lack capital.

For Stage 1 companies, it is all about being pro-active, having a smart plan, establishing a solid foundation and being aware of your resources to capital. Access to capital has changed dramatically in the past few years. To avoid the issues that come with undercapitalization, plan your approach.

In the past, most startup businesses were self-funded through personal savings (credit cards, home equity, lines of credit, etc.). The second tier of resources comes from bank loans, loans or "gifts" from family, employees, partners and friends.

> Disclaimer: all businesses are different, and therefore the levels of capital and the pace the funds will be expended will always fluctuate. The goal here is to outline the best practices for almost any business starting out, or in the throes of Stage 1.

There are a couple of tips that are vital to your Smart Plan.

Tip #1: **It is always best to have capital resources "in advance" of when your business needs it.**

There are few worse things for a business than when you start to feel the pinch of cash flow. It makes all decisions tougher. This symptom shreds your attention level and restricts your business's potential.

Tip #2: **Avoid depleting your personal financial resources before seeking financing.**

You may think it is wise to go as far as you can before taking on debt. But consider how you will look to a lender when they ask for a personal financial statement. They want to see available equity, cash and cash equivalents. Debt, when used wisely, is a business's best friend. A bank will likely want a personal guarantee and if there are limited assets and cash, it makes the transaction unlikely. Small business bank loans are based on a lender believing in you and your ability to carry out a plan that will provide repayment of the loan.

There are four major pathways to funding, other than self-funding through family and friends.

1. STANDARD BANK DEBT FINANCING

You will meet with one person during the courting process to secure a bank loan. Your friendly business development officers have a job and that is to fill their pipeline with opportunities. They are sincere in their interest to help your business, however they are not the decision makers.

Once an application and all of the appropriate documentation is provided, the bank turns the data over to a credit-underwriting specialist. Their job is to meticulously analyze your submittal and poke holes in it. They are sensitive to risk. A low credit score, a tax lien or inconsistent tax returns are big red flags. The other big red flags relate to bankruptcy filings and unfulfilled obligations (defaults) to other banks.

Here are some of the key criteria banks use to further their understanding of your business and the opportunity.

Surveying the Landscape:

- You, the current business and your payment history.
- Purpose of the loan and the amount requested; relationship to any current debt.
- Type of loan (equipment, lease, line of credit or general business loan).
- Sources of repayment.
- Competition.
- Covenants and controls the bank can impose.

Elements of Good Underwriting:

- Your competency, character, management and leadership experience.

- Business type and industry considerations (predictability, cyclical nature and current stability).
- The business and personal collateral: ratio to loan and risk, liquidity, ability to control your business, contingency risk. In the case of default, the bank's ability to establish possession.
- Remedies and ability to keep the business and ownership on track.
- Risk and return consideration.

Hiding or not reporting bad news on your application is very unlikely to go unnoticed. Banks share data. They have access to a depth of information on your personal credit. Don't waste time, it will only come up later and you will lose credibility.

To maximize the value of a bank loan for your business, talk with a few different banks and then ascertain which one you can imagine creating a good working relationship with. You can demonstrate your goodwill and receive their willingness to assist through pro-active communication.

2. SBA LOAN PROGRAMS

The SBA has a number of programs for different types of companies. Shown below is a summary of the different programs and their focus, percent of guaranty, benefit to borrowers and who is qualified.

SBA U.S. Small Business Administration
QUICK REFERENCE TO SBA LOAN GUARANTY PROGRAMS

Program	Maximum Loan Amount	Percent of Guaranty	Use of Proceeds	Maturity	Maximum Interest Rates	Guaranty Fees	Who Qualifies	Benefits to Borrowers
7(a) Loans	$5 million	85% guaranty for loans of $150,000 or less; 75% guaranty for loans greater than $150,000 (up to $3.75 million maximum guaranty)	Term Loan. Expansion/ renovation; new construction, purchase land or buildings; purchase equipment, fixtures, lease-hold improvements; working capital; refinance debt for compelling reasons; seasonal line of credit, inventory or starting a business	Depends on ability to repay. Generally, working capital & machinery & equipment (not to exceed life of equipment) is 5-10 years; real estate is 25 years.	Loans less than 7 years: $0 - $25,000 Prime + 4.25% $25,001 - $50,000 P + 3.25% Over $50,000 Prime + 2.25% Loans 7 years or longer: 0 - $25,000 Prime + 4.75% $25,001 - $50,000 P + 3.75% Over $50,000 Prime + 2.75%	(No SBA fees on loans of $150,000 or less approved in FY 2014.) Fee charged on guaranteed portion of loan only. $150,001-$700,000 = 3.0%, $700,000- $1,000,000 = 3.5%; plus 3.75% on guaranty portion over $1 million. Ongoing fee of 0.52% on loans over $150,000.	Must be a for-profit business & meet SBA size standards; show good character, credit, management, and ability to repay. Must be an eligible type of business. Prepayment penalty for loans with maturities of 15 years or more if prepaid during first 3 years. (5% year 1, 3% year 2 and 1% year 3)	Long-term financing; improved cash flow; Fixed maturity; No balloons; No prepayment penalty (under 15 years)
7(a) Small Loans is any 7(a) loan $350,000 and under, except the Community Advantage and Express loans	$350,000	Same as 7(a)	Same as 7(a)	Same as 7(a)	Same as 7(a)	Same as 7(a)	Same as 7(a). All loan applications will be credit scored by SBA. If not an acceptable score, the loan can be submitted via full standard 7(a) or Express.	Same as 7(a)
SBAExpress	$350,000	50%	May be used for revolving lines of credit (up to 7 year maturity) or for a term loan [same as 7(a)].	Up to 7 years for Revolving Lines of Credit including term out period. Otherwise, same as 7(a).	Loans $50,000 or less, prime+ 6.5% Loans over $50,000, prime + 4.5%	Same as 7(a)	Same as 7(a)	Fast turnaround; Streamlined process; Easy-to-use line of credit
SBA Veterans Advantage 01/01/14 - 09/30/14	Same as SBAExpress	Same as SBAExpress	Same as SBAExpress	Same as SBAExpress	Same as SBAExpress	No guaranty fee Ongoing fee of 0.52% on loans above $150,000.	Same as 7(a). Plus, small business must be owned and controlled (51%+) by one or more of the following groups: veteran, active-duty military in TAP, reservist or National Guard member or a spouse of any of these groups, or a widowed spouse of a service member or veteran who died during service, or a service-connected disability.	Same as SBAExpress; No guaranty fee
CapLines: 1. Working Capital; 2. Contract; 3. Seasonal; and 4. Builders	$5 million	Same as 7(a)	Finance seasonal and/or short-term working capital needs; cost to perform; construction costs; advances against existing inventory and receivables; consolidation of short-term debts. May be revolving.	Up to 10 years, except Builder's CAPLine, which is 5 years	Same as 7(a)	Same as 7(a). Plus, all lenders must execute Form 750 & 750B (short-term loans)	Same as 7(a). Plus, small business must be able to meet SBA 7(a) eligibility requirements.	1. Working Capital - (LOC) Revolving Line of Credit 2. Contract - can finance all costs (excluding profit). 3. Seasonal - Seasonal working capital needs. 4. Builder - Finances direct costs when building a commercial or residential structure
Community Advantage Mission-focused lenders only. Expires 03/15/17	$250,000	Same as 7(a)	Same as 7(a)	Same as 7(a)	Prime plus 6%	Same as 7(a)	Same as 7(a)	Same as 7(a). Plus lenders must be CDFIs, CDCs or micro-lender targeting underserved market

U.S. Small Business Administration
10 S. Howard Street, Suite 6220
Baltimore, MD 21201

Baltimore District Office
(410) 962-6195
www.sba.gov/md

Information current as of March 2014
SBA Programs and services are provided on a nondiscriminatory basis.
See the SOP for the most up to date detailed information

To download the Quick Reference to SBA Guaranty Program, use this link: www.bizchallenges.com/referenceSBALoans

3. CROWDFUNDING

Now a significant player in the world of small business enterprise funding, crowdfunding is used for a multitude of businesses and creative endeavors that otherwise would be left without a path to cash. The website, www.massolution.com, put out a report indicating that crowdfunding raised approximately 2.7 billion in 2012, and was expected to grow by almost double in 2013.

There are two main models for Crowdfunders. The first is donation based funding. Donors contribute in respect to a collaborative goal, in return for products, perks or rewards. The second model is the investment approach.

Some key sites to consider:

- Kickstarter: creative-based, donation funding focused on the arts, film and video, dance, photography and journalism.
- Startup Crowdfunding: a global crowdfunding service to connect startups, crowd investors and business angels in over 150 countries. Used as a conduit to attract more serious business investors. They claim to have 100,000 profiles and 20,000 investors.
- Crowdfunder: solely an investment funding vehicle, Crowdfunder is a strong player in crowd investment funding. Generally funds mid to large amounts for businesses.
- RocketHub: offers a "success school" and best practices pathways to generate interest in your initiative. All types of products and businesses are listed. RocketHub is strategically aligned with A&E Project Startup, a group that searches RocketHub to bring your product to life.
- appbackr: focused on early seed, donation-based funding solely for mobile apps, using their campaign tool, Marketplace. A showcase for the very best apps. It also provides an "appscore," a predictive analytical ranking system, scoring on intrinsic quality, user traction and sentiment.
- AngelList: established for tech startups with a significant lead investor in place. Predominantly Silicon Valley, geo-centric based opportunities. (Must also be incorporated in Delaware.)

- Quirky: a collaborative portal for donation-based crowdfunding if you are an inventor. Quirky offers a community to move the needle on progress.
- Peerbacker: donation funding for all types of projects; most are smaller scale in nature, but there are also a number of mid to larger scale. (A 5% success fee is charged for funds raised.)
- MicroVentures: a crowdfunded investment bank. They conduct detailed due diligence on startups and, if approved, they help raise capital from angel investors. They are a FINRA registered broker dealer. Main areas of interest are: Internet technology, media and entertainment, software, green tech, mobile, social and gaming.

4. ANGEL FUNDING

Instead of going to an aggregator like MicroVentures, AngelList or Startup Crowdfunding, you can also seek capital the old-fashioned way and reach out to the Angel Club in your area.

Why are they called Angels? Because they are people who have earned their nest egg and are ready to give back. Angels enjoy the process of being engaged in something they have an interest in, or someone they see as investment worthy.

Generally, their primary motivation is to be engaged as a mentor throughout the startup process. John May, of New Vantage Group, wrote a book called, *Every Business Needs an Angel*. He does a great job of illuminating the motivations and value propositions the right Angel can bring to your business.

Angel participants may pool their resources on one company. Investors will want to see a local Angel or lead investor geographically near your business. Start to think locally.

Angels typically are the seed funding and early round funding source; they come in after your personal investment has occurred. Their investment range can be as low as $25,000 and as high as $800,000 (possibly even higher).

THE VALUE OF IDENTIFYING FUNDING OUTLETS

There has never been a better time to be a borrower. Low interest rates, a large, active and well-prepared investment community and an improved economy succeeding in a weaker global system prove this. Remember, the U.S. entrepreneurship pool is likely the best-trained group ever.

> There has never been a better time to be a borrower.

In 1983, there were six schools dedicated to the pursuit of degrees in Entrepreneurship. Today, there are over three thousand. If you believe you could use some online education on starting your company, go to the FastTrac section at www.kauffman.org, which has provided training to more than 300,000 entrepreneurs.

Your job as a Stage 1 business leader is to have accurate personal financial statements, a passion for what you do and the time to pursue those investors most likely to be interested in your offering.

RESOLVING THE CHALLENGE OF HAVING LIMITED CAPITAL TO GROW

Having limited capital to grow for a Stage 1 owner doesn't have to be related to a large infusion of cash. If you think about capital as a resource you want to preserve and spend wisely, or if you think about capital as your time and energy and you allocate it efficiently, you will build a successful business.

Having limited capital to grow can negatively impact growth at all stages; not just in terms of reaching specific indicator targets (such as the number of clients, revenues, profits), but also in the long view that takes the company beyond its immediate vision. If an organization is working with a product that is time sensitive to the market, a lack of capital will hinder it from day one.

As a startup business looking for outside investment capital, the CEO will need help creating a solid business plan. An investment business plan designed to help raise capital is far different in content than an operational business plan.

THE TOOLS YOU NEED TO RAISE MONEY:

- A one to two page summary stating the year founded, industry, product or service and location of the business.
- This document should also cover the funding strategy, management team, strategic advisors and other useful information.

- The main content should include the problem, your solution, target market, competitors, competitive advantage, marketing strategy and your revenue model.
- It is a benefit to generate detailed two-year sales and expense projections, footnoting key issues and assumptions made to the plan. It is essential for you to be honest about the threats to your plan. Having realistic numbers is well received compared to the "hockey-stick" look to sales and profits. Show months of slower cash intake and higher expenses. Sensitizing your numbers to the variables all businesses face enhances serious consideration.
- If you are presenting to Angels, you will need a concise 10-15 slide deck that covers the key points to tell your story. Many times the Angel will have a certain format they wish to be used.
- Last is an executive summary (four to six pages) to lead your investors in a narrative format to know more about the opportunity, your value proposition and why you and your team are going to be successful.

As you move through the process, you may need a full-blown business plan, but early on, this will get your business the attention from viable investment resources.

Working with a strategy and business planning professional will bring out the best at this critical stage and allow you to focus on day-to-day activities. The money spent on the front end will more than pay for itself.

Challenge #5: Expanding Sales

Expanding sales is a challenge typical for startups. Why do so many small businesses falter out of the gate and wind up shutting the doors? Often, it's because there is a lack of *vision*, a lack of commitment for success and a lack of future planning.

Expanding sales starts with a clear vision of what problem you are solving and for whom. It starts with a belief that your product or service is so good, so much better than your competitors that you are just dying to create proof of concepts with anyone who will buy what you offer.

> Expanding sales starts with a clear vision of what problem you are solving and for whom.

Expanding sales is one of a business owner's biggest roles, especially in a Stage 1 company. You are the best promoter of what you offer. It's your passion and enthusiasm that makes people buy from you in the early stages of development.

"But I hate sales! I just want to create my product or deliver the service. I hate the sales aspect of running my business." Does this sound like you? If so, you need to get over it.

You have to sell in the beginning, even if you have the resources to hire ten sales people out of the gate. Your ability to lead your people down the right sales path will influence how well your company grows at all stages of growth.

EXERCISE #1:

UNDERSTAND THE SALES PROCESS

Successful companies are those where the CEO has taken the time to immerse himself in the problem-solving aspects of the product or service and is able to articulate those problem-solving aspects to potential customers. If the CEO can do this, he can teach others to do it.

Identify and articulate a sales process that can be replicated by anyone in the organization. Start by answering these questions:

- What is your attitude about sales?
- Are you, the business leader, a good sales person?
- What inaccurate or negative beliefs do you carry that might be influencing your attitude about sales?
- Do you know how to build rapport with a prospect?
- Are you a good listener?
- Do you ask good questions?

- Are you focused on the prospects and solving their issues, or do you just talk about your benefits and features?
- Do you have a strong lead generation process?
- Is there a defined and proven sales process?
- Do you understand how your company solves a customer's problem?

If you need help with sales, get it. Don't assume you can just wing it. Too often, we think price will be the driving force behind a prospect making a decision, so please see the Five Steps of the Buying Decision.

You need to create a relationship with someone before they will "know, like and trust" you. Take the time to get to know people and their needs before you launch into your product or service offering. Nothing is more annoying than meeting someone for the first time who immediately launches into a 30-minute sales pitch. Listen to what people have to say about what they do, where they struggle and what they might be looking for help with. Enjoy the conversation and enjoy connecting. Let people get to know you, and during that conversation, you'll find ways to share who you are and what you do.

> Take the time to get to know people and their needs before you launch into your product or service offering.

FIVE STEPS OF THE BUYING DECISION

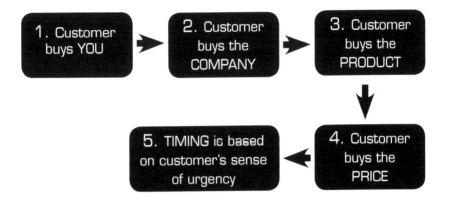

THE SEVEN STEPS OF THE SALE

There are lots of sales experts in your industry so I recommend you do your research. I've outlined a beginning process that can get you started.

1. Approach – Establish bonding and rapport, get a prospect to "know, like and trust you."
2. Interview and Upfront Contracts – Set expectations and determine objectives of a meeting.
3. Understand Their Pain – What is the problem, why is it a problem, what is the impact of the problem, what have they done recently to solve the problem?
4. Refine and Listen – Explain your solution as it addresses the pain, listen for objections.
5. Budget – Is the prospect willing and able to make an investment to solve his pain?

6. Getting to Decision – What is the buying process for the prospect? Ask for a decision.
7. Follow-up – Walk your talk. Don't allow buyer's remorse to set in. Explain next steps.

THE VALUE IN UNDERSTANDING THE SALES PROCESS

It's not unusual in a Stage 1 company that the owner is the sales person. The company is likely too small to have a sales team and who knows the product or service better than the person who designed it?

As a company grows, the CEO will want to build a sales team. However, unless he has captured his process and can teach it to others, he will always be the best, and sometimes only, effective sales person. More often than not, this becomes a huge obstacle to growth. The CEO needs to be involved in many other aspects of the operation; those activities will take him away from sales. If no one else is prepared to handle sales for the company, it will not survive.

By clarifying the sales process, a CEO will be able to recognize good salesmanship practices. This will come in handy when he is ready to hire the first sales person. If you already have a sales team, make certain you are the driving force behind their plans, their processes and their quotas.

Too often business leaders disconnect from sales believing someone with more experience can run this part of the business. From a skills point of view, that may be correct. From a knowledge point of view, the business leader can add valuable insight that should always be a part of the sales program.

EXERCISE #2:

DEFINE YOUR VALUE PROPOSITION FOR EACH PRODUCT OR SERVICE YOU SELL

A value proposition is a promise of value to be delivered. It's the primary reason a prospect should buy from you. In a nutshell, a value proposition is a clear statement that:

- Explains how your product solves customers' problems or improves their situation (relevancy).
- Delivers specific benefits (quantified value).
- Tells the ideal customer why they should buy from you and not from the competition (unique differentiation).

A value proposition is a short statement that clearly communicates the benefits that your potential client gets by using your product, service or idea. It boils down the complexity of your sales pitch into something that your client can easily grasp and remember.

It needs to be very specific. Simply describing the features or capabilities of your offer is not enough. Your value proposition must focus closely on what your customer really wants and values. Your customer wants to solve problems, to improve on existing solutions, to have a better life, build a better business or do more, better, faster, etc.

WHAT MAKES A GOOD VALUE PROPOSITION:

- Clarity! It needs to be easy to understand.

- It communicates the concrete results a customer will get from purchasing and using your products and or services.
- It differentiates you from the competitor.
- It avoids hype (such as "never seen before, amazing, miracle product"), superlatives ("best") and business jargon ("value-added interactions").
- It can be read and understood in about five seconds.

Work with your staff to really understand what problems you are solving for your prospects and gear all interactions with those prospects to help them see you as the provider of their solution.

Our value proposition for product/service A is:

Our value proposition for product/service B is:

Our value proposition for product/service C is:

THE VALUE IN DEFINING YOUR VALUE PROPOSITION

You must have clarity of the *why,* in terms of why your product or service helps solve customer problems, if you want your employees to engage in what they are delivering. Once your employees truly understand why your products or services solve customer's problems, they'll be able to identify how what they do every day helps the company to grow and deliver on your value proposition.

EXERCISE #3:

DEFINE YOUR MARKETING MESSAGES

Develop your marketing messages early. Talk to people who have actually bought your product or service and capture their testimonials. Without well thought out, consistently executed marketing efforts, your sales pipeline will dry up. Marketing fuels sales, so it's not an option; it's a must have.

Create a marketing plan. Make it a priority. Commit to creating a marketing plan for each product or service offering, as they likely have different target audiences, different goals and objectives and require different strategies. There are a lot of resources that can provide great input on how to develop and execute a marketing plan. In Dallas Murphy's book, *The Fast Forward MBA in Marketing*, he reminds us, "The marketing concept holds that business activity is the process of creating a satisfied customer (i.e. making a market) and that profit is the reward for doing so."

Here are the essentials. It's easy for an entrepreneur to be completely focused on the product or the service and forget the one reality that will make or break his success: Does that product or service solve a problem, for whom and how? If it's a great product or service but no one needs it, it will not last. Make sure you are aware of how each of your products or services solves a problem

> **Commit to creating a marketing plan for each product or service offering.**

and create your marketing messages and your plans around the "WIIFM – What's In It For Me" approach.

> Our marketing plan for product/service A is:
> Our marketing plan for product/service B is:
> Our marketing plan for product/service C is:

IDEAS TO CONSIDER FOR YOUR MARKETING PLAN

1. Gather intelligence – Where are you now in your marketing awareness? Do you know who your customers are? Do you know what their pain is? Do you know how your product or service addresses that pain? Who are your competitors? How are you different from them? How does your market perceive you today?

2. Set goals and objectives – Determine where you want to be and when. Make your goals realistic, but a stretch. What will your return on investment look like? Where are you starting and what results do you want?

3. Identify your marketing mix – Are you going to use direct mail, trade shows, advertisements, social media, public relations? In addition to identifying your marketing mix, you need to create a budget and a schedule for each strategy. Create key indicators so you can measure how well each strategy is doing.

Ensure that you have marketing initiatives planned and scheduled at least six months in advance.

- Are there marketing avenues you have not tried before or should consider trying again?
- How can you improve your lead generation system?
- How can you ensure that more leads are turned into customers?

THE VALUE IN DEFINING YOUR MARKETING MESSAGES

Knowing how well your product or service is being received by your customer is the best way to evaluate your marketing activities and effectiveness. If they answer your questions about your product and use the words and terminology from your marketing materials, you know you hit their pain points and your words resonated with them.

RESOLVING THE CHALLENGE OF EXPANDING SALES

The key to this challenge is to *focus* on the sales process. Focus on what it is you are selling and focus on how it will solve problems. Then find as many opportunities as you can to shout about these wonderful attributes to the world.

Do you have a website? Don't think that just because you have built it, they will come. If you expect your website to help drive sales, it needs to be a sales-driven website, rather than an online brochure that talks in vague terms about what your company does.

Are you a networker? Approach networking with a strategy. Select only those groups that are your target audience and find contacts you can build into relationships that will end up in sales. Be intentional about how you spend your time exposing people to your product or service.

You can't generate sales without a solid marketing plan. Evaluate what's in your marketing mix and if you need help, go get it. You don't have to spend thousands of dollars, but you do have to be clear about which marketing approach will drive the most sales to your business in the short and long term.

> You can't generate sales without a solid marketing plan.

You have to spend time in your own head figuring out how your product or service solves your target audience's problems. This could simply mean sitting and spending some quiet time clearly outlining the benefits of your offering. It doesn't have to be costly or complicated.

What's Next?

The great thing about understanding your challenges upfront is that you can work on them immediately and move on! You don't have to worry about where to devote your time and you have a clear outline of how to move your company from 1-10 employees to 11-19 employees.

Business owners who have the ability to focus on the right things at the right time build successful businesses. If you make sure that you are working on these five challenges every day, your company will respond and reward you with results.

Many business owners are not able to put words to their issues. They simply know there are issues hitting them every day and they *react* to each issue separately, depending upon how critical the issue is at that exact day and hour. Reacting to issues is not an effective way to grow a business. Understanding your key issues, identifying them and working on them is a formula for success!

As a company grows, so must the leader. Each stage of growth will require something different. Understanding what is required of you as your company evolves can either propel the company forward or cause the company to stagnate: profits never materialize, sales suffer and there is high employee turnover.

> **As a company grows, so must the leader.**

Unlocking the profits in a Stage 1 company with 1 – 10 employees starts when you hire that first employee and make your first sale. Laying a solid foundation for growth today will ensure your success tomorrow.

A client and good friend had this to say after I worked with him for a couple of years and introduced him to the 7 Stages of Growth:

> *"Laurie, I've been reading the same old recycled business ideas for years and have been looking for a fresh perspective — and this is it! Tapping into your research, insight and knowledge should be an A1 priority for all business leaders. I especially like that you have your message broken down based on stage of growth. Too many of the gurus out there are writing 'one size fits all' prescriptions that don't apply to companies of different sizes. After all, implementing the right thing at the wrong time is guaranteed failure. So thanks again for really understanding what we need to hear and presenting it in such a way that we can use it to make a direct impact. I'm definitely going to tell my non-competing CEO friends about you."*

> David Paulson, CEO, Accuer, Boulder, CO

Survival is the name of the game in a Stage 1 company. As you move closer to Stage 2 (11 – 19 employees) the priority shifts to growth. Stage 2 is about supporting higher sales levels and making a profit.

The bottom line in understanding the 7 Stages of Growth is that the complexity of an organization will always extract its due.

Are you ready to tackle Stage 2 Challenges? My book, *Sales Ramp Up: How to Kick Start Performance and Adapt to Chaos with 11-19 Employees,* offers tips on how to address the top five challenges for the second stage of growth.

Take a look at our website, www.bizchallenges.com, for additional products and services for business owners who are passionate about turning their growing business into a great business.

FOUNDATION BUILDING BLOCKS FOR STAGE 1 BUSINESS MODEL

REFINE A SIMPLE BUSINESS MODEL LAYING OUT THE COMPANY'S:

1. Value propocition
2. Target customer/channel
3. Product/service features and pricing
4. Revenue streams
5. Marketing and sales strategy
6. Operations strategy
7. Profitability
8. Cash flow

SALES

Experiment until the company discovers its unique value proposition that resonates with target clients. Develop a simple sales system that works and can be replicated and used by all salespeople.

FINANCIAL SYSTEMS

Financial systems should include:

1. A simple financial model to understand what affects the bottom line
2. Cash flow forecasting and tracking
3. Profit planning spreadsheet

PROCESSES

Identify and document key processes. Train staff so they understand the processes.

PEOPLE

Start identifying the qualities you want in an exceptional employee. Hire the right people and trust them. Define clear outcomes. Meet weekly with each employee to get to know who they are and uncover the best way to help them achieve those outcomes.

* *

STAGE 1 AND NOT A STARTUP: 1 – 10 EMPLOYEES

There are companies that choose to stay in Stage 1. Their business plan operates well with under 10 employees, generating enough income to provide a good living for the CEO as well as the employees. With the advent of the Internet, Internet companies are small, agile entities that can drive a lot of revenue with very few people. There are also many brick and mortar companies that continue to thrive and not move out of Stage 1.

With that said, one of the key messages driven from the research of the stages of growth, is "If you aren't growing, you're dying." So even a 20-year old retail shop will start seeing an erosion of profits, clients moving away, market share dwindling if they don't do something to continue to refresh their business goals and objectives. A company who has been in Stage 1 for a good length of time may need to reach out to a new market, open a new location, expand its product or service offerings. Something will have to ignite their growth and keep their revenue and profit alive.

A STAGE 1 COMPANY AT A GLANCE

CEO-CENTRIC

Number of Employees:	1 – 10
Number of Managers:	0
Number of Executives:	1
Builder/Protector Ratio:	4:1

Three Gates of Focus:

Profit

People

Process

Three Faces of a Leader Blend:

Visionary	40%
Manager	10%
Specialist	50%

Leadership Styles:

Visionary

Coaching

Commanding

ARE YOU READY FOR STAGE 2?

The real value in understanding the 7 Stages of Growth lies in the ability to predict what's coming; to see around the corner, if you will. Stage 2 has 11 – 19 employees. You are no longer just trying to survive; you now have a real business, that you need to ramp up for sustainable growth.

As a CEO looking at your growth plan and knowing that you will breach that 11th employee in just a few months, if you are a student of the 7 Stages of Growth, you already know three things:

1. Your top challenge is hiring quality people.
2. Your top gate of focus continues to be Profit and your second gate of focus is Process.
3. Your leadership style moves from Visionary to Coaching.

With just those three pieces of knowledge, you can start thinking about your hiring process and asking yourself, "Are we prepared to ramp up our ability to hire good people?" You can start thinking about what makes a good hire for your company. Better yet, you can start asking your employees why they enjoy working for you and start capitalizing upon your reputation as a growing organization that cares about its people.

You can also start evaluating your processes – few as they may be – and asking yourself, "Should we be looking at adding critical processes as we add more people?" You can evaluate what has been working, what is no longer working and begin to engage your employees in capturing best practices. You can begin the education of your team as to the value of good processes, not just for process-sake but in order to be more efficient, to help your employees work smarter, not harder.

And you can begin to learn the value of a Coaching leadership style, which helps you become an efficient delegator and assign employees challenging tasks, two skills that will serve you and your company well as you continue to grow.

> Staying ahead of your growth curve reduces chaos, puts more money on your bottom line and helps you stay ahead of your competitors.

Moving from a Stage 1 company to a Stage 2 company means you have fine-tuned your offering, solidified your value proposition and offered your customers solutions that have them coming back for more. It also has you growing beyond your capacity to make all of the decisions, handle all of the sales, and manage every employee.

While there are many similarities between a Stage 1 and Stage 2 company, there are important differences as well.

The real test for a Stage 2 leader comes as you react to having less control and more employees. When your role as Manager increases, your role as Specialist decreases. You are now looking around your growing organization realizing that your idea has matured and now, so must the company.

Watch for Laurie's next book in her 7 Stages of Growth book series – *How To Kick Start Performance and Adapt to Chaos with 11 – 19 Employees.*

ADDITIONAL RESOURCES

Buckingham, Marcus and Coffman, Curt: *First Break All the Rules*

Fischer, James: *Navigating the Growth Curve: 9 Fundamentals that Build a Profit-Driven, People-Centered, Growth-Smart Company*

Flamholtz, Eric G. and Randle, Yvonne: *Growing Pains*

Goleman, Daniel; Boyatzis, Richard and McKee, Annie: *Primal Leadership: Realizing the Power of Emotional Intelligence*

Maxwell, John C.: *The 21 Irrefutable Laws of Leadership*

O'Berry, Denise: *Small Business Cash Flow*

Stack, Jack: *The Great Game of Business*

Welsh, Jack: Jack: *Straight From the Gut*

Wheatley, Margaret J.: *Finding Our Way: Leadership For an Uncertain Time*

White, Karyn Ruth: *Dream Droppings: An Entrepreneurs Field Guide*

Wilkerson, Carrie: Barefoot Executive: *The Ultimate Guide for Being Your Own Boss & Achieving Financial Freedom*

May, John: *Every Business Needs an Angel*

HIRE LAURIE AS A SPEAKER!

Laurie Taylor has spoken to thousands of business audiences. Her topics include organizational growth, using the 7 Stages of Growth as a foundation, leadership development and employee engagement.

CRACKING THE CODE TO YOUR COMPANY'S GROWTH –

Challenging insights into how companies grow based on a unique research study that shows the complexity level increases as you add people. Knowing your stage of growth provides predictability about growing a business that you can't find anywhere else.

YOUR PEOPLE ARE YOUR BUSINESS –

The biggest challenge we face as business owners is the management of people. We all know people leave managers, not companies. If you address the reality of "your people are your business" early on in your company, managing profitability, performance and productivity will be easier. Learn how to break down barriers that exist between managers and employees and create relationships that engage and encourage employees to excel.

EVERYTHING RISES AND FALLS ON LEADERSHIP –

Who are the leaders in your organization? Is leadership improvement an intentional part of your company's culture? John Maxwell, the voice of leadership and author of over 70 books on the subject, identified five levels of leadership – Position, Permission, Production, People Development and Pinnacle. Learn how to apply these principles and extend your own influence as a leader to build a culture of responsibility and authenticity.

You can reach Laurie at **laurie@igniteyourbiz.com.**

LAURIE'S CLIENT TESTIMONIALS:

"Before I tallied the evaluation forms, I knew that you were a hit! You were able to appeal to a group of business owners and top executives who are diverse in their industries, in their stage of business and in the sizes of their organizations. As I mentioned to you, this market has many one-person businesses, but I also have some of the largest employers in the region as members. You addressed the entire range with great success."

- Ken Keller, STAR Consulting

"Successful business owners will usually figure it out, but often only after it has become a problem. The Navigating the Growth Curve model is uncanny in its ability to accurately predict what is about to happen to business owners, so they can act before it costs them time, emotional energy and money.

As for Laurie Taylor, I gave her a real challenge: give a three-hour presentation to 35 business owners and senior executives. The real challenge? They represented every conceivable size and type of company from startups to Fortune 50, from law firms to manufacturing to technology companies. Laurie nailed the presentation giving tremendous value to everyone in the audience. After three hours, these top executives were still in their seats and taking notes. Now that is impressive!"

- Bill McIlwaine, Renaissance Executive Forums

"Laurie's presentation received rave reviews at our annual professional conference. Several attendees commented that she was the 'best value' in the entire conference, and 'worth the price of admission!' Here are other comments we received. Great presentation!"

"Laurie was excellent. She was worth the price of the entire conference."

"By far the BEST presentation at this conference. Laurie's dynamic, real, humble and confident."

"Outstanding! I would take it again!"

"Stars! Worth the cost of coming here alone. Extraordinary."

"The best value in the entire CMI conference."

"Very motivating and engaging, as well as a good reminder of essentials."

"Bring this one back next year."

- Susan Whitcomb, Career Masters Institute

"Laurie's program is credible because she has been through growing a business as a business owner. Her presentation offered succinct tips on how to focus on my business."

- Will Temby, Greater Colorado Springs Chamber of Commerce

"Very informative and extremely eye opening! I really appreciated Laurie's honesty in talking about her own mistakes as a business owner."

- Jon Hicks, Hicks Benefit Group

"*Laurie Taylor conducted a 4-hour workshop on the Stages of Growth for 30+ company CEOs, plus several of their management team. She effectively walked the entire group of companies to a clear understanding of this dynamic business model. In addition, she facilitated exercises that allowed the CEOs and their executives to begin to map out plans on how to manage their businesses. She had all parties engaged throughout the workshop.*

Prior to being exposed to the Stages of Growth, some of the companies were like bumper cars bouncing around with limited forward motion, focusing on the non-important issues. The Stages are the GPS of business growth in that they provide clarity, focus and direction. Several companies that attended are now implementing the tools and processes that will lead to growth and improved profitability.

I recommend Laurie Taylor and the Stages of Growth to any business entity."

- Tony Hutti, Executive Forums

ACKNOWLEDGEMENTS:

This book has been a vision of mine for years. I wrote it with the hope that, in a small way, it will help us to reverse the trend of so many small businesses failing within the first five years. Small business has been, and can be again, the economic engine we need to create jobs.

My thanks go out to the people I've worked with and who have been a part of my circle of friends and business associates. I appreciate their counsel, their friendship and their support.

Ralph Crozier, from Strategy Plus, for his guidance, his help with developing the content, his constant encouragement and his belief in me, which took an idea I'd had for three years and helped me turn it into a reality. www.strategyplus.net

Brooke White, my editor, whose skills and insight were invaluable in editing and pushing me to add critical pieces of information the reader will benefit from. I appreciate her patience and her experience.

Kim Hall, from Inhouse Design Studio, who created the front and back covers and layout for the book. Her creativity helped make the book come alive. www.inhousedesignstudio.com

James Fischer, for his research on the 7 Stages of Growth and his focus on the small business owner.

My clients over the years, who have taught me so much and allowed me to be their trusted advisor.